WOMAN and HOME

SIMPLE FLOWER ARRANGING

WOMAN and HOME

SIMPLE FLOWER ARRANGING

Carolyn Bailey

HAMLYN

First published in Great Britain in 1994
by Hamlyn
an imprint of Reed Consumer Books Limited
Michelin House, 81 Fulham Road,
London SW3 6RB
and Auckland, Melbourne, Singapore and
Toronto

First paperback edition 1995

Art Director	JACQUI SMALL
Executive Editor	JUDITH MORE
Art Editor	LARRAINE SHAMWANA
Editor	JENNY JONES
Production	ALISON MYER
Design	MAGGIE TOWN & BOBBY BIRCHALL
Illustrations	JANE HUGHES

ISBN 0 600 58746 0

A catalogue record for this book is available from
the British Library

Printed by Mandarin Offset
Printed and bound in China

Contents

Introduction

I adore flowers, whether they are blooming in the garden, or cut and arranged in a vase indoors. With the intensity of their colours and the fragility of their blooms, flowers bring a place to life. They cheer you up, and offer a daily source of pleasure as new buds open to reveal subtle variations of shape and colour.

In this book I have tried to share my love of flowers, and to provide inspiration for colour themes and styles. These range from cottagey displays – try my all-time favourites of sweet peas, scabious and larkspur – for that time of year when the shops are full of frothy pastel blooms, to ideas for dried flower arrangements that prolong the flower season almost indefinitely. Sculptural displays are included too, which are especially suitable for the dormant period when you will find plenty of bright red gerberas, bold lilies and colourful roses at the

florists just waiting to be arranged. All too often we buy flowers as presents, and feel it is indulgent to keep them for home. Why not do the opposite ... and purchase flowers for yourself as often as possible! You don't necessarily have to get in lots of material from the florists. Sometimes just a few carefully chosen blooms provide heaps of pleasure.

It's so easy to be put off flower arranging for fear of getting it wrong, or not knowing where to start. The emphasis in this book is on simplicity. You don't need any specialist tools – often all that is required is a couple of bunches of flowers, some foliage and a bit of imagination. If you follow a few guidelines and keep the displays simple, you really can't go wrong. Don't be afraid to experiment, and don't worry too much about which flowers go together and which clash. Take nature as your inspiration,

OPPOSITE A mixture of lady's mantle, Queen Anne's lace, astrantia, trachelium and asters fill an enamel bread bin and ceramic pot.

LEFT Foliage supports a mixture of daffodils and irises with golden yellow stripes.

BELOW A medley of alstroemerias, scabious, feverfew, lady's mantle, lavatera, hydrangeas and a sprig of New Dawn fill a vase that has been covered with florist's moss.

where blooms in all hues and shapes successfully mingle together. The colour sections in the book will give you a starting point on which to build your ideas for colour combinations.

If you are buying flowers from a florist, select blooms that are in bud with some colour showing. Always get them home as quickly as possible, especially in hot weather. The moment you get indoors plunge them into a bucket of lukewarm water and allow them to drink to their heart's content – for at least a couple of hours. Once they have had their fill you can re-cut their stems – make diagonal cuts, allowing the widest possible surface area to absorb water. Then

RIGHT Flowering bulbs create a colourful display for a console table.

arrange. If you plan to mix narcissi with other blooms, cut their stems to length in advance, and place them in a vase on their own for at least 24 hours. This way the slime they emit (which can be harmful to other flowers) will disperse, saving other blooms from an early demise.

I love using flowers and foliage from the garden for my displays, firstly because it's so convenient, and secondly because I enjoy seeing the flowers closer to hand. By mixing garden-grown foliage with just one bunch of shop-bought blooms you can end up with a

splendid arrangement. Unfortunately, flowers from the garden don't generally last as long as florist's blooms, which are specially bred for cutting. But you'll find that just a few marigold or sweet pea plants will keep you in fresh flowers throughout the summer.

It is lovely to buy flowers for a specific vase, but if you don't have one in mind, don't worry. I hope the section on containers will inspire you to use more unusual choices such as kitchenware and even vessels made from fresh fruit and vegetables. Choosing or decorating a

ABOVE Ready and waiting – bunches of colourful blooms just asking to be arranged.

ABOVE A window box filled with narcissi, Pinocchio striped tulips and red ranunculus makes a brilliant table display for lunch parties.

OPPOSITE A trug stained blue and lined with plastic is the perfect container for hyacinths, crocuses and primulas.

container is all part of the fun, and it's an important element of the overall display.

Always place your flower arrangement in a spot where you can see and appreciate it. Even if you like having flowers in your sitting room, it may be better to place them in the hallway where you will see them more often – and what better way to be greeted when you open the door on your return home. I always make sure I have a seasonal display on the window sill in my kitchen – even if it is just a simple bunch of flowers casually arranged – as it is usually one of the

first things I see in the morning and one of the last things I see at night.

Arranging flowers can be incredibly rewarding. And if you look after the blooms carefully, you will find that the display will last surprisingly well. To make sure that you get the most from your flowers, be sure to study the pages on care and conditioning of your plant material (see pages 100-103).

Life just wouldn't be the same without flowers. So go on, experiment, be bold and, above all, enjoy creating a work of beauty.

Containers

ABOVE Snapdragons, Queen Anne's lace and gomphrena create an eye-catching display in a green bowl.

OPPOSITE Wide-necked containers such as this large urn vase will require a mist of blooms such as sweet peas, stocks, love-in-a-mist and aquilegias.

The container you choose for any flower arrangement is vitally important, as it plays an integral part in the overall success of your display. Always try to visualize how your vase and flowers will go together before starting an arrangement. For maximum flexibility, keep a wide range of containers in all shapes, sizes and colours close to hand.

Your choice of flowers will, of course, affect your choice of container – sculptural flowers are well matched by modern vases with sleek lines, while masses of country-style blooms look at home in rustic-type containers made of wood or wickerwork. Long-stemmed flowers sit happily in tall vases, while small blooms prefer to nestle in shallow bowls. You can get away with the minimum of blooms in a vase with a narrow neck – just a few slender stems will look impressive. However, beware of wide-necked containers – they usually need a profusion of flowers to make any impact.

A useful way to create a more generous effect with a bunch of flowers is to support the stems in wire mesh at the bottom of the vase.

ABOVE Shallow bowls need small, fragile flowers such as polyanthus to fill them. Use the leaves as well as the blooms.

Or fix sticky tape across the top of the container to support the blooms and to prevent them from falling over the sides.

The surroundings that provide the setting for your arrangement will also affect your choice of vase. Modern interiors call for containers with more architectural forms, while warm terracotta and wickerwork are better suited to a country-style setting.

There are no hard-and-fast rules about the size of flowers that should go in specific containers. But, generally speaking, your arrangement should be about one-and-a-half times the height of your container. Having said that, some flowers look best when their stems are cut right down so that their blooms just peek over the edge of the vase – try carnations, anemones, roses and even larger blooms such as lilies.

Glass vases are the most versatile type of containers for flower arrangements, so always keep a few at the ready. They blend well with almost any kind of display, setting the blooms off to their best advantage. The stems can also look very pretty in the vase, and you can add

LEFT Snip off a couple of blooms from potted pansies for a breathtaking arrangement in a china teacup and saucer.

marbles or pebbles for extra interest. Make sure you remove all unsightly foliage that falls below water level. This operation will also help to keep the water clean and make sure that plant material lasts as long as possible.

You can present your flowers in almost anything that holds water. Look out for interesting alternatives to traditional vases. Lots of kitchenware such as jugs, teapots and drinking glasses make interesting containers. Jars, bottles, galvanized buckets and watering cans are also surprisingly versatile. You can disguise the most unsightly of vessels by wrapping it with fabric, leaves or moss. A terracotta flowerpot with a jar placed inside it also makes an excellent container, and can be decorated with water-based paint for a coordinated scheme.

Hollowed-out fruit and vegetables, such as melons and small pumpkins, provide unusual and interesting "vases". Simply place a smaller glass or vase inside the organic container and use this to hold the flowers – you won't be able to see the inner container once the flowers have all been arranged.

BELOW A medley of brightly coloured dahlias are arranged in a simple glass vase hidden in a wicker basket.

RIGHT Repot begonia plants into a wicker basket lined with plastic, then cover the soil with a layer of moss.

OPPOSITE Boldly coloured polyanthus are an excellent match for a rustic container.

– Types of Containers –

Gather together containers in a mixture of different materials: pottery, china, glass, basketware, stone, metal and wood are all good choices for holding flowers.

China containers offer a wide selection for your displays; and because you can't see the flower stems and water, you can provide support for stems in the form of wire or plastic mesh, florist's foam or even a few twigs and no-one will ever know. If the container is patterned, choose flowers in complementary colours. Light-coloured vases work well with frothy displays in pastel hues, such as scabious, sweet peas and stocks. Bold vases need an equal match. Combine tulips in primary colours or brightly coloured roses with strongly decorated vessels. Look out for pretty teacups and saucers, which are ideal for blooms with short stems. Shallow bowls are good for small flowers too, especially for the many short-stemmed

RIGHT Single sprays of rosehip, blackberry and old man's beard are offset by sunny marigolds in an old urn for holding cream.

spring flowers. Snip off some polyanthus blooms and leaves, for example, and fill a bowl to overflowing. Place the bowl on a matching plate for a striking table centrepiece (see page 16). China jugs, urns and mugs also make excellent makeshift containers.

Wickerwork or basketware are excellent containers for rustic-style floral displays. As almost any colours work well with these materials, you are spoilt for choice when it comes to selecting flowers to go with them. Generally speaking, wickerwork looks good with traditional arrangements. Fill simple baskets with a myriad of the same blooms – dahlias, for instance, work brilliantly in this kind of arrangement, as the wickerwork will not detract from the intensity of the blooms.

When arranging cut flowers in a wicker container, hide a smaller vessel filled with water inside it. And wickerwork doesn't have to be left plain. Use a water-based paint diluted with

water and then lightly brush the solution over the surface. It will transform the basket magnificently (see page 74).

Metal containers can set off your flowers beautifully, and all sorts of metal containers are on offer to the flower arranger. The only drawback with metal surfaces is that they can sometimes appear cold. Combat this by a clever choice of blooms in rich colours to give the display warmth. Old or antique containers such as copper mixing bowls and pans, which have wonderfully mellow tones, provide a sumptuous foil for warm-coloured displays – choose the reds and pinks of chrysanthemums and hydrangeas for a stunning effect. Old pewter items make great vessels for floral displays in deep, jewel-like colours. Look out for beaten tankards in antique shops and try a small display of deep, dusky-coloured anemones. Silver containers are always an elegant choice. Keep them sleek and shiny with regular cleaning, or leave

LEFT Rosehips, pyracantha berries, sprays of blackberries and oats combine effectively with apricot chrysanthemums, late hydrangea blooms and a selection of mahonia and hydrangea leaves.

them to become lightly tarnished for a more interesting effect.

Do double check that your chosen metal container is completely waterproof before placing the finished arrangement in position. There is nothing worse than a trickle of water, especially if the display is sitting on a favourite piece of furniture. Take the safe way out and put a small glass vase filled with water inside the container. Metal does have one advantage over other types of containers. Because it is a naturally cold material, metal will keep the water and flowers cool. And the cooler the display, the longer it will last.

Once you have chosen your container, the next important decision is where to position it. It helps if you have a favourite spot for your arrangement each week. Even if you do, consider changing any ornaments or other items nearby in order to create a still life.

It's very rewarding to find a new and different container that sets off your favourite flowers to perfection. Don't be afraid of the unusual – it can work brilliantly.

23

Designs for Colour

BELOW Repot forget-me-nots into a wicker basket lined with a plastic bag for a display on a window ledge.

OPPOSITE Take an urn vase, some multi-coloured parrot tulips and you have the formula for a fabulous display.

One of the most exciting aspects of flower arranging is choosing what colours you are going to use. The choice is limitless, and – best of all – there are no hard-and-fast rules about which colours do and don't work well together. It's entirely up to you, your mood and your personal taste. Take a look at the colours in nature and you'll see that anything goes. The time of year may well influence your choice of blooms, however. Although you can now get almost any flowers at any time of the year, it's often best to stick to seasonal flowers for home arrangements. They work out better value for money and you can be sure that they are in the best possible condition.

The colours readily available also alter with the seasons. For example, in the northern hemisphere, spring is most associated with yellow and blue – the colours of grape hyacinths, hyacinths and daffodils. Summer brings a glorious mixture of soft and bold shades, while autumn or fall offers a myriad of warm reds, russets and golden browns. Then there is winter, which boasts rich colours and a wide variety of evergreens – yew, spruce, cypress and laurel.

When choosing flowers, take into account your colour scheme at home. As a general rule, choose soft shades for neutral or pastel rooms, and opt for bold colours in brightly decorated interiors. If you mix bold with soft, the bold colours will dominate the gentler shades, and their subtlety will be lost.

Your choice of container will also dictate what colours you select. Glass, wickerwork and terracotta containers are all ideal choices if you don't want to be tied down to any particular hue. But if you have a brightly painted jug, for instance, it's fun to match it with equally colourful flowers.

You can play safe by going for a single colour, using either the same flowers or several varieties in slightly different shades of the same colour. Another popular combination is to stick to two different colours. At the other end of the scale, mix and match every colour under the sun in one big, flamboyant display.

There is nothing more rewarding than discovering a pleasing floral combination. Experiment, be adventurous – you won't be disappointed in the results.

Red

BELOW *A few bunches of stocks brimming from a pitcher make a wonderful display.*

RIGHT *Arrange sweet peas in vases with narrow necks to show off their delicate beauty.*

—— *Pretty Pinks* ——

Pink flowers ranging from the palest of pale blooms to the rich, deep hues of magenta are all-time favourites. Walk into a flower shop at any time of the year, from spring to the depths of winter, and you are bound to find a good selection of pink flowers.

When florists are bursting with buckets of pink ranunculus, hyacinths, freesias, tulips, and delphiniums a small but effective display can be made using just one bunch each of freesias and ranunculus. Tulips look striking on their own or can be mixed with foliage such as the lovely gray-green leaves of eucalyptus. For something a little different, look out for parrot tulips, which have blooms with delightful frilly edges. There are also several varieties of tulips around with sharply pointed petals, which make a lovely change from the the usual type. China Pink has delicate slim petals in a very pretty shade of pink, and there are lots of other colours available. You might even be lucky enough to track down one of the varieties of tulips that have exquisite two-tone petals to fill a simple vase or jug.

You can now buy hyacinths as cut flowers too. They survive well in water, but they last even better in their traditional form, potted in compost. The best thing about hyacinths, of course, is their delicious smell, which will fill your home with a glorious scent.

The arrival of lilies in all different shades, peonies, sweet peas, snapdragons, cornflowers dahlias, gladioli, stocks and astilbes are always welcome. Many of these can be grown in the garden and mixed with shop-bought flowers. Flowers with long, sinewy stems, such as sweet peas, are seen at their best arranged in a vase with a narrow neck so that they can spread out above the vase, making a very pretty fan-like display. Again, sweet peas will fill the house with their delicate perfume.

When sedums, garden roses, asters, hydrangeas, statice and berries appear, all shades of pink come into their own. Even when your

BELOW An old decanter picked up in an antique shop provides an ingenious makeshift vase for a bunch of sweet peas.

OPPOSITE Jugs make generous containers for plentiful blooms. This pink and purple display sums up the very best that the height of the growing season has to offer – love-in-a-mist, peonies, delphiniums, scabious, and, of course, sweet peas.

LEFT Frothy herbs such as soft thyme and marjoram blooms make a perfect foil for pink cornflowers.

BELOW This arrangement brings together beautifully coloured foliage and late-flowering roses.

NEXT PAGE Asters come in all shades of pink and purple. They are a cheerful sight and blend well with eucalyptus leaves. A jar is the perfect container for a couple of large hydrangea heads.

favourites are not available, you can rely on gerberas and other all-season flowers such as carnations for a good range of pinks.

A mass of pink looks heavenly on its own. Use a mixture of pink flowers in a variety of shades to give your display texture and depth. Pink blooms also happily blend in with flowers in other colours. Pink and purple are particularly captivating together – try brilliant pink ranunculus with purple hyacinths. Herbs with purple blooms are lovely studded with pink cornflowers. Blue and pink is another superb combination – lots of blue cornflowers and scabious studded with pink garden roses always looks ravishing.

There is nothing nicer than the colour pink offset by the strong greens of garden foliage. It's a good way to make your blooms go further, and you'll have a magnificent display with just one bunch of shop-bought flowers. Although strong red and yellow are striking together, it's best to avoid putting yellow and pink together; they seem to fight with rather than complement one another.

A Riot of Red

BELOW Shells provide unusual containers. Just a couple of blooms plucked from the garden – roses, scabious, busy lizzies and cornflowers – make a simple but dramatic display.

OPPOSITE Sometimes you will only need a few flowers to make an impact. Placed in a simple glass vase, who could ignore these striking gerberas?

Bold, brash and vibrant – bright red and deep, luscious pink flowers make stunning arrangements you can't ignore. If you are using strong, hot colours, you can get away with using fewer flowers than usual. Just a couple of blooms – large roses and gerbera, for instance – will create an impressive display.

Orange comes into this dazzling category too, and will never disappoint, especially when the garden is brimming full of marigolds,

poppies and nasturtiums. They all make wonderful cut flowers, and will bring a touch of sunshine indoors. (Garden marigolds will flower more profusely if you cut the blooms regularly – deadhead any you have missed.) Mix them with purple, yellow or blue for a really bold display. Red is extremely plentiful throughout the autumn months, with several shrubs producing bright red berries. Scarlet is, of course, *the* colour at Christmas time.

Warm pink sedums, the last of the garden marigolds and a mass of foliage are turned into a brilliant display.

Russet Brilliance

Russet-coloured flowers, ripening fruit and end-of-season foliage take on a brilliance quite unlike that of any other. To re-create this arrangement, put rich reds together with vibrant pinks and oranges. Partner crab-apples, rosehips and hawthorn berries with ornamental vine leaves, and use suitably coloured flowers to provide a bold focal point.

You will need: 2-3 stems each mahonia leaves, rose foliage, ornamental vine leaves; 3-4 stems each fruited crab-apples, dog rose with hips, hawthorn with berries; 3-4 each dark-eyed marigolds, sedums, helichrysum, pelargoniums; 2-3 stems fuchsia.

34

1 *Start your display by arranging the foliage. Use a mixture of mahonia and rose foliage and ornamental vine leaves to form the basis of the arrangement.*

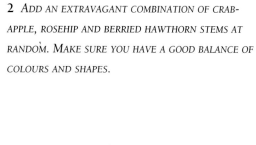

2 *Add an extravagant combination of crab-apple, rosehip and berried hawthorn stems at random. Make sure you have a good balance of colours and shapes.*

3 *For dramatic effect, place a few dark-eyed marigolds, sedums, helichrysum and shocking pink sweet-scented pelargoniums at the front of the arrangement. Pop in a few stems of gently drooping fuchsia flowers to finish.*

A mist of dried pink and cream blooms, arranged in a glass vase lined with sweet smelling pot-pourri, makes this two-in-one display extra special.

Pink Surprise

Reminiscent of the flowering months, this glorious dried arrangement of complementary blooms is a wonderful sight that will last and last. If that's not enough, the glass vase is brimming full of richly scented pot-pourri that will excite your sense of smell too. Any damaged blooms can be intermingled with the pot-pourri to save waste.

You will need: A glass tank vase, block of florist's dry foam cut to size, small bunch dried pink roses, small bunch dried helichrysum, small bunch dried button flowers, small bunch dried everlasting flowers, generous bunch dried batao and grasses, mixed petals and pot-pourri to line vase.

1 *CUT YOUR BLOCK OF DRY FOAM HALF THE HEIGHT OF THE VASE AND 1CM (½IN) SMALLER THAN THE INTERIOR OF THE VASE.*

2 *ARRANGE THE LARGEST FLOWERS, SUCH AS THE ROSES AND HELICHRYSUM, FIRST. THESE WILL FORM THE OUTLINE OF THE DISPLAY.*

3 *ADD A FEW OF THE SMALLER BLOOMS AT RANDOM, THEN SOME MORE LARGE FLOWERS. FILL GAPS WITH BATAO AND GRASSES.*

4 *HIDE THE FLORIST'S DRY FOAM BY LINING THE VASE WITH MIXED PETALS AND POT-POURRI. THESE CAN BE LAYERED IN CONTRASTING COLOURS FOR THE BEST EFFECT.*

Yellow

RIGHT Buttercups and Queen Anne's lace, fresh from the garden, are a true country combination, especially when arranged in an enamel jug.

—— *Mellow Yellow* ——

The myriad of blooms in soft shades of yellow are fresh and cheerful. Throughout the year, the choice of yellow flowers is endless, starting with the muted tones of primroses to favourites that include freesias, lilies, roses and solidaster. Yellow blooms can stand alone, but they often look better mixed with other colours such as cream and blue. For a country-style display, try mixing buttercups with Queen Anne's lace; for something more sophisticated, combine yellow roses and freesias with white yellow-flagged irises. Solidaster, which has tiny yellow blooms, is a very useful filler for yellow displays and lasts extremely well as a cut flower. For something out of the ordinary, why not make a globe of flowers from cheerful yellow chrysanthemum blooms using a ball of wet florist's foam soaked in water. Snip off the flower heads, leaving 7cm- (3in-) stems, then insert them into the foam until it is covered in a mass of blooms.

LEFT Freesias, yellow roses, white irises and solidaster make an impressive display in this ceramic pitcher.

BELOW Late flowering roses blend well with yellow spray pompon chrysanthemums and tansy flowers. Mixed green foliage – quince, vine and blackberry leaves – frame the display.

OVERLEAF You can bring a bold splash of colour into your home with yellow lilies, jasmine and roses mixed with viburnum.

39

—— Yellow Bright ——

There is nothing retiring about some yellow flowers. Take yellow tulips and ranunculus, for instance. They have bright, multi-petalled blooms that positively sing out. Sunflowers are attention grabbers too. They are getting more and more popular and you can now buy miniature versions as well as the familiar large flower heads. These blooms are so impressive that just a few stems placed in a large container will instantly make an impact. Large yellow roses and lilies are good mainstays too.

All bold yellow flowers are outstanding bunched together in a display consisting of a single variety, or try mixing them with other species that have yellow blooms. Introducing another strong colour into a yellow scheme adds a new and exciting note to the arrangement. Throw in some vivid blue or purple and the yellow flowers will appear to stand out even more. And for a really striking arrangement, try yellow with bright red.

Bulbs in Yellow

Probably the best loved yellow flower from a bulb is the daffodil. You can choose from so many varieties. Some smell delightful, and others surprise with their exquisite two-tone blooms. There are miniature versions that have small, delicate heads, while other varieties possess showy double blooms. This versatile bulb is easily repotted into a range of attractive containers, especially trugs and baskets. Simply line your container with a sturdy plastic bag before repotting. Add grape hyacinths, or a couple of polyanthus, to complete the display. Daffodils also make superb cut flowers. Mass them together in a celebration of glorious yellow, or arrange them with tulips and foliage. There is a slight problem with cut daffodils, however, in that they emit a slime from their stems that is harmful to other cut flowers placed in the same container (see page 103 for details on how to overcome this).

RIGHT Repot narcissi and grape hyacinths into a painted trug for an impressive display that will last and last.

OPPOSITE Just a few bunches of daffodils fill a jug with bold blooms.

Bright yellow and orange flowers are a zingy colour combination and are guaranteed to bring a ray of sunshine into your home. The colour theme is continued by the orange kumquats placed inside the vase.

Flowers and Fruits

If you love glass vases but are tired of seeing the flowers' stems, here is an unusual and attractive solution – simply hide them with fruit! Despite the golden rule "don't mix fruit and flowers" (if you do put them together, the fruit may *slightly* reduce the life of the flowers), this is a real winner for a special occasion. Who can resist the combination of bright orange kumquats, halves of limes and a glorious selection of floral material?

You will need: Glass vase, sufficient kumquats and limes to fill vase, 5 stems ruscus, 3 stems yellow lilies, 5-6 yellow roses, 7-8 yellow and orange marigolds, 7-8 carthamus, 4-5 sprigs solidaster, 5 ranunculus.

1 *Fill the vase with plenty of fresh, luke-warm water. Add several kumquats and some lime halves at random.*

2 *Arrange the ruscus foliage, taking great care not to dislodge the kumquats. A few branches will give the arrangement shape.*

3 *Once you have formed the outline of the display with the foliage, start to add a few yellow lilies, evenly spaced.*

4 *Add a mixture of yellow roses, yellow and orange marigolds and orange carthamus. To soften the display use several sprigs of soli-daster. Position a few ranunculus blooms at the front so that they can droop over the edge of the vase, softening its rim.*

47

Bring the best of the seasonal foliage and golden-hued flowers together. Use a range of artificial flowers for a truly everlasting display.

Golden Days

This potent arrangement is a mixture of yellow helichrysum, bronzy foliage and gray-green eucalyptus. Artificial flowers such as silk lilies and roses provide accents of colour.

You will need: Block of florist's dry foam cut to fit; gravy or cream boat; 6 stems dried bracken; 4-6 each dried stems maple and sycamore; small bunch dried polygonum; small bunch dried moluccella; 5-6 stems dried eucalyptus; 4 dried ornamental yellow chillies; small bunch dried alstroemeria; small bunch silk single chrysanthemums; small bunch silk roses; 4 silk lilies; small bunch dried helichrysum.

1 *FILL THE CONTAINER WITH A BLOCK OF FLORIST'S DRY FOAM CUT TO FIT. CREATE THE OUTLINE FOR THE DISPLAY USING A MIXTURE OF FOLIAGE, LEAVING AMPLE SPACE FOR THE OTHER PLANT MATERIAL.*

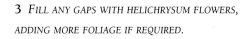

2 *ADD DRIED EUCALYPTUS, AND THE LARGER YELLOW FLOWERS.*

3 *FILL ANY GAPS WITH HELICHRYSUM FLOWERS, ADDING MORE FOLIAGE IF REQUIRED.*

Blue

BELOW An exhilarating display of narcissi, primulas, hyacinths and grape hyacinths prove that blue and yellow are a wonderful mixture.

Barely Blue

Flowers in soft shades of blue are cool and calming, and their presence in flower arrangements brings a lovely, serene touch. Blue has a tendency to recede, however, if it is placed next to a more dominant colour. To ensure that blue flowers stand out, keep the display simple and either stick to different shades of blue, or add white or yellow blooms to provide a gentle contrast. The delicate blues range from the palest sky blue to subtle lilacs and mauves, and there's a good range of flowers to choose from in these pastel hues. Select from hyacinths, delphiniums and irises; consider anemones, cornflowers and scabious; and don't forget Michaelmas daisies, heathers and thistles. Some blue flowers such as love-in-a-mist are easy to grow from seed in the garden or a window box, and flower profusely during the growing season.

ABOVE A wicker basket filled with generous bunches of heather is studded with toning artichokes.

LEFT White stocks set off the blue of veronicas and corn-flowers beautifully. Blue cornflowers work well with white freesias.

51

True Blues

PREVIOUS PAGE A bold collection of purple anemones, pink hyacinths and purple irises will never fail to please.

RIGHT Dried produce, including delphiniums, thistles, helichrysums, achilleas and a selection of greenery, make for an unbeatable floral display.

OPPOSITE Here is an arrangement that doesn't need any extra help. Simply fill a vase with a selection of blue, mauve and pink delphiniums – voilà!

ABOVE Orange and purple is a magical combination. A jug filled with a mixture of garden marigolds and lisianthus make a bold statement.

Blue needn't mean pale. Some of the boldest flowers that are available come in brilliant blues. Delphiniums, for instance, come in a variety of shades ranging from a whisper of blue to an almost unbelievably deep sapphire. Cornflowers are often a very striking blue too. Arranging such intensely blue flowers is simplicity itself. Mass them together in a single vase and instantly you have an impressive display. Strong blues are an equal match for vibrant red, orange and yellow flowers, although the lighter, hotter colours will always be the more dominant hues. Try deep lilac lisianthus with bright orange marigolds.

Dried flowers extend the blue season. Look out for dried delphiniums and purply thistles to arrange with dusky yellow flowers such as golden-coloured helichrysums and achilleas. Lavenders, heathers, cornflowers and larkspur are also excellent for permanent displays.

Bulbs in Blues

So many flowers for indoor planting come in varying shades of blue. Take grape hyacinths. They are not only a delight growing in the garden, but they also look fantastic indoors grouped together in a special pot of their own. Crocuses are also a good choice for an indoor bulb in blue or purple, as are irises.

If you long to fill your home with a rich scent, choose hyacinths. Repot them into a suitable container, such as a china bowl or a rustic basket, and use a layer of sphagnum moss to hide the soil.

Ideally, potted bulbs should be kept in cool conditions, and watered little and often if the container has no holes for drainage. Over watering will reduce the length of flowering. If you prefer multi-coloured displays, mix blue-flowering bulbs with narcissi and pink or yellow polyanthus. Foliage plants, especially ivy, are attractive with bulbs.

OPPOSITE Repot a couple of pots full of flowering crocus into jolly ceramic bowls

BELOW The spires of grape hyacinths grow up and out from a simple china bowl.

A glass jug in a frosted deep blue is the ideal container for a colourful arrangement of purply blue anemones and irises, blue eryngium, creamy yellow freesias and narcissi and eucalyptus foliage.

Fresh Blue

Flowers come in so many different shades of blue that it's difficult to decide on which to use in a display. Ideally, go for a few of your favourites. Here, wonderful purple-blue irises streaked with yellow are combined with anemones and eryngiums. Blue is particularly effective when combined with blooms in soft yellow and creamy shades. Here, pale-coloured freesias and narcissi provide gentle accents. Use several stems of small-leaved eucalyptus to soften the overall effect.

You will need: 14 stems small-leaved eucalyptus, 3 stems eryngium, 9-10 purple-blue irises, 5-6 anemones, 5 freesias, 4-5 narcissi.

1 *CREATE THE SHAPE OF YOUR DISPLAY WITH A FEW STEMS OF SMALL-LEAVED EUCALYPTUS, THEN POSITION 1 OR 2 STEMS OF ERYNGIUM TOWARDS THE BACK OF THE CONTAINER.*

2 *ADD THE BLUE FLOWERS FIRST, STARTING WITH A FEW IRIS BLOOMS, THEN ADD THE ANEMONES. KEEP SOME OF THE STEMS LONG AND CUT OTHERS TO DOWN TO NESTLE AT THE FRONT OF THE DISPLAY.*

3 *BREAK UP THE EXPANSE OF BLUE WITH A FEW PALE YELLOW FREESIAS, THEN ADD SOME NARCISSI STEMS HERE AND THERE. (TO PREVENT THE STEMS OF THE NARCISSI EMITTING SLIME THAT MAY REDUCE THE LIFE OF THE OTHER FLOWERS, CUT TO THE REQUIRED LENGTH AND LEAVE THEM TO SOAK OVERNIGHT ON THEIR OWN IN A BUCKET OF WATER BEFORE ARRANGING.) FINALLY, ADD A FEW MORE STEMS OF EUCALYPTUS TO FILL ANY GAPS.*

This rustic twig basket sets off the beauty of preserved red roses and the richness of dried lavender. Together they combine to great effect – and the smell of the lavender will fill your home.

Touch of Drama

The contrast between the vibrant colours in the display and the simplicity of the rustic twig basket gives this arrangement considerable impact. The rich, dark red roses are complemented by the deep purple lavender, while greenery softens the whole. Relatively few flowers are required for this display, so it is easy and cheap to make.

You will need: 20.5cm (8in) diameter basket, block of florist's dry foam cut to fit, 14-15 dried red roses, generous bunch dried French lavender, generous bunch dried greenery, florist's adhesive tape.

1 *Fill the basket with a block of florist's dry foam cut to fit. Use florist's adhesive tape to secure the block if necessary.*

2 *Cut the stems of the roses to the height of the handle on the basket to determine the height of the display. Then arrange at frequent intervals.*

3 *Fill the areas between the roses with greenery and lavender until you have an even effect.*

White

— Elegant Whites —

White is one of the most versatile "colours" available to the flower arranger. White flowers look good in most containers – everything from earthy terracotta pots to bold blue and white china. White flowers are also stunning displayed in a white vase.

An all-white floral display is one of the most classic of flower arrangements – use plenty of dark green foliage as the perfect foil to the white blooms. White flowers range in colour from icy white to cool shades tinged with green or blue and warmer hues with a hint of pink or yellow. They are all ideal for informal and formal displays throughout the seasons.

Make the most of white flowers, from the first of the snowdrops, tulips and crocuses, to favourites such as gladioli, roses and stocks. Combine them with small white flowers – soapwort gypsophila, feverfew and dill – for a generous, massed effect that is also light and frothy.

RIGHT Plant white snowdrops closely together in a tureen and group with white and yellow crocuses in matching china.

OPPOSITE White soapwort softens the spires of white and pink gladioli.

OVERLEAF A glorious mixture of lilies, miniature roses, orchids, lisianthus, love-lies-bleeding, foliage, apples and berries form a breathtaking display in a vase covered with bark and tied with raffia.

BELOW Bridal gladioli, single spray chrysanthemums, spray carnations, white roses and stocks, beautifully offset by a wide selection of foliage, make a superb formal arrangement in a low vase.

RIGHT A mass of white blooms are all the ingredients you need to create a dramatic display.

OPPOSITE You'll only need a few stems of lilies to fill a large vase. Add eucalyptus leaves to fill the gaps.

— White on White —

White flowers can be extremely dramatic. Large, graceful lilies, such as the trumpet or Easter lily, for instance, are majestic in any display. Stately on their own, you can always add some foliage such as a few stems of gray-green eucalyptus to soften everything. Used alone, generous bunches of pure white tulips are another striking single colour arrangement. Their translucent petals are beautifully offset by their slender pea-green leaves.

White flowers reflect the light, so they are the perfect candidates for placing in dark corners. They are also an excellent choice for dinner parties, as the petals will stand out in the glow of candlelight.

You are spoilt for choice when it comes to creating a bold, dramatic effect using white flowers. Look out for orchids, amaryllis, arum lilies, dahlias, gladioli, larkspur, lisianthus and, of course, roses.

— Hints of White —

Many white flowers come tinged with subtle shades of pink, yellow, green or blue. These give an extra dimension to an arrangement in white, and will often dictate its mood. A hint of green or blue gives a cool, collected air to any display; the same in pink or yellow adds a touch of warmth. Think of roses, which come in every imaginable shade of white, dahlias, freesias, chrysanthemums, asters, anemones, snapdragons and delphiniums.

OPPOSITE *A few stems of chrysanthemums and snapdragons are softened with Queen Anne's lace and asters.*

ABOVE *Roses and wax flowers combine beautifully with the variegated leaves of euphorbia.*

LEFT *Blossom and narcissi create a fresh yellow display.*

69

Sometimes the most unusual containers are the most successful. This wine carrier might have been designed to hold jars, which in turn provide excellent makeshift vases for floral displays.

White Delight

An all-white display can have a spellbinding effect, especially if it is placed in a dramatic setting. Here, to avoid detracting from the beauty of the blooms, the flowers are arranged in a wicker six-bottle wine carrier. A jar has been placed in each of the six separate sections to provide individual floral displays that look like one. The handle of the basket helps to support the stems of the flowers and makes a good spot for trailing ivy.

You will need: Wine carrier with six sections, six jars, few stems eucalyptus, few trails ivy, 5-6 white anemones, 10 freesias, 6-8 chincherinchee, few stems Queen Anne's lace, few stems buttons flowers, few sprays asters.

1 *FILL THE JARS WITH LUKEWARM WATER. PLACE THEM IN THE WINE CARRIER, MAKING SURE THAT THEY ARE SECURE.*

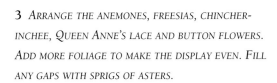

2 *THE FOLIAGE — EUCALYPTUS AND IVY — PROVIDES THE FRAMEWORK FOR THE BLOOMS. BEGIN BY ARRANGING THE EUCALYPTUS. CUT SPRIGS TO THE HEIGHT OF THE BASKET HANDLE AND ARRANGE A FEW OF THESE IN EACH JAR. PLACE A FEW TRAILS OF IVY AT THE FRONT AND SIDES OF THE BASKET.*

3 *ARRANGE THE ANEMONES, FREESIAS, CHINCHERINCHEE, QUEEN ANNE'S LACE AND BUTTON FLOWERS. ADD MORE FOLIAGE TO MAKE THE DISPLAY EVEN. FILL ANY GAPS WITH SPRIGS OF ASTERS.*

An impressive array of grasses towering above a simple terracotta pot turns simplicity into elegance.

Country Look

Dried grasses blend harmoniously with the earthy tones of a terracotta flowerpot. This display makes a feature of their long rigid stems by arranging them in a simple fan shape so that they stand bolt upright in the container.

You will need: 18cm (7in) diameter terracotta flowerpot; block of florist's dry foam cut to fit; handful each sheaves of wheat, straw, barley, avena and briza; generous bunch *Achillea ptarmica* "The Pearl"; all-purpose adhesive; off-white paper ribbon.

1 *Three-quarter fill the flowerpot with florist's dry foam. Use a sharp knife to trim off the edges for a good fit.*

2 *Arrange the grasses in a fan shape, making sure you get an even mix of varieties.*

3 *Glue on a couple of rows of Achillea ptarmica "The Pearl" to frame the outer rim of the pot.*

4 *Tie on a large off-white paper bow and glue it in place at the front of your display. Adorn with a couple of sprigs of grass to finish.*

Mixed Hues

ABOVE Queen Anne's lace, scabious and bright red poppies fill a cobalt blue jug.

RIGHT Lilies, old-fashioned roses, feverfew, astilbes, trachelium and phlox form a soft display in a painted wicker basket.

Softly, Softly

There is a wonderful array of floral colours available to the flower arranger, and the choice of colour combinations is never ending. Apart from the many superb hues available in Nature, flower breeders are constantly adding to our choice with new and different manmade shades. Fortunately, there are no rules as to how you should go about putting colours together, and this is certainly true for all the soft colours. They don't clash, generally speaking, so you can mix them up to your heart's content. Just choose the flowers you like and experiment with fresh and exciting colour schemes.

Gently muted shades are everywhere at the height of the flowering season, and they look marvellous grouped together in an assorted display – for starters, try pink, blue, cream and lilac. Select these colours in roses, lilies, feverfew, trachelium, phlox and button flowers and arrange them in a rustic basket. Sweet peas come in an exquisite range of delicate colours; try mingling them with pinks and cornflowers.

BELOW pinks, sweet peas, Achillea ptarmica "The Pearl" and cornflowers make a sweet display in a small glass bowl.

OVERLEAF Sunflowers stand out boldly against red dahlias, lisianthus blooms, hot pink accents of gomphrena, eucalyptus and euphorbia.

— Mix and Match —

Don't be afraid of mixing several bold colours together. The effect can be sizzling. If you are using flowers straight from the garden, mixing and matching in this way is a very economical approach to creating an impressive display without completely ransacking any one bush. Simply pluck a few blooms from here and there, then put them together – you will be amazed by the results. Ideally, try to ensure a good visual balance in the arrangement – if a particular colour is dominant, it will take over and detract from the other blooms. For a harmonious display, always try to mix your chosen colours in equal quantities.

The time of year will to some extent dictate the choice of colours available. Blue, yellow and cream are found together in one season, while pink, blue, cream, yellow, red and purple are the colours most closely to hand at another. You may find hot shades of orange,

blue and red at the same time, or vivid reds and greens with startling whites. There are several flowers which are available all year around from florists, such as roses, chrysanthemums, lilies and gerberas. Try mixing them together ... just this once.

Garden flowers – larkspur, marigolds, delphiniums, rose of sharon and roses – were made for bold mixed arrangements. Keep the containers simple, or make them yourself by hollowing out pieces of fruit such as the large melon shown here.

Some flowers, such as poppies, zinnias, dahlias, roses and ranunculus, come in all sorts of colours – take one species in a range of colours and mass them together or take a colour and use this as the starting point for a display that consists of several varieties in similar tones.

Use lots of foliage to break up a dramatic mixed arrangement. Many of the blooms available from florists have little or no leaves, and you may well have to buy foliage separately. Try laurel leaves, arching stems of eucalyptus, or a few sprigs of trailing ivy.

OPPOSITE TOP A garden medley that includes lisianthus, larkspur, alstroemerias and roses stand proud in an urn.

OPPOSITE BOTTOM Red roses, Californian lilac, rose of sharon and marigolds are displayed in a melon shell.

ABOVE Gerberas and irises look great in a wicker basket.

— Two's Company —

Creating an arrangement in a myriad of hues takes a sure eye and a confident hand. If you are not quite ready for this, displays that are limited to two colours are equally as effective, and quicker and easier to put together. You can either choose two colours that are related, such as red and orange, green and blue, and pink and purple; or try the complementaries: red and green, orange and blue, and yellow and violet. You can arrange them bunched together in the same container, or display them separately in a mixture of vases. If you keep the containers small, ideally with narrow necks to support the flower heads, you won't need much floral material. Just a couple of gerberas, for instance, look striking. Or try arranging marigolds and small sunflowers in glass drinking vases. Another source of inspiration for a floral twosome is the container itself. Any colourfully decorated china is an excellent starting point.

BELOW Red and yellow flowers – gerberas, ranunculus, marigolds and anemones – are a bold combination placed against a green background.

OPPOSITE Match the colour of the flowers to that of the container. Here, marigolds, cornflowers and a single sprig of anethum continue the rich blues and yellows of the jug.

—A Medley of Bulbs—

Bulbs offer a spectacular choice of colour combinations. Daffodils, hyacinths and tulips are always a cheering sight, and come in all shades, from bright yellow and orange to blue and red – all musts for your indoor potted arrangements. Hyacinths can be grown in traditional hyacinth glasses, which are specially designed to hold an individual bulb above water so that the roots can grow down to drink plenty of fresh water. To add interest to the display, try growing hyacinths in a transparent glass vase filled with a layer of pebbles. Water them regularly and watch the roots grow in and around the pebbles.

Flowering bulbs are always available from garden centres, and it's easy to repot them yourself into pretty containers. Try china bowls, wicker baskets, or even a bark container. If the container isn't waterproof, line it with some thick plastic sheeting first. As an alternative, place a non-porous container inside your chosen vessel. It's always good to have a couple of pots of narcissi replanted into pretty bowls for a bright show – choose scented varieties if you also want to fill the room with a delicious smell. These can be grown successfully in your kitchen and then planted out in the garden so that they can flower the following year too.

Potted freesias and anemones are also popular, which is not surprising when you consider their extensive colour range and lovely shapes. Freesias will fill your home with their distinctive, sweetly peppery aroma, and anemones, although scentless, are worth their weight in gold when it comes to introducing gorgeous splashes of colour into the home.

If you want a change from bulbs in the more traditional shades of brilliant yellow and cobalt blue, it's worth considering those that come in soft shades of cream, peach, pink and pastel blue: you will find a wide range of hyacinths and gladioli in these hues.

ABOVE Use a glass container to grow hyacinth bulbs.

RIGHT Repot bulbs into an interesting container such as this bark planter.

OPPOSITE Sometimes the simplest displays are the most effective. Narcissi fill a steel bucket and a primula sits in a miniature watering can.

The last of the garden roses, rich harvest fruit and foliage provide a wonderful display.

Rustic Splendour

A large inglenook fireplace is the ideal setting for this superb mixture of fruit and flowers displayed in a rustic basket. The basket contains pink, apricot and white roses with leafy stems of hawthorn, japonica, buckthorn and elder; old man's beard gives interesting texture, while pomegranates and red and yellow crab-apples add bright touches of colour.

You will need: Shallow but wide basket, plastic liner; block of florist's wet foam cut to fit; 3-4 stems buckthorn; 4 stems old man's beard; 10 stems selection pink, apricot and white roses; 6 stems crab-apples; few stems hawthorn; few stems japonica; few stems elder leaves; 2-4 pomegranates.

1 *Line the basket with a plastic bin liner and put in the florist's foam cut to fit. Dampen with water. Start to arrange the buckthorn and old man's beard. Keep the foliage at the back long to give the display height. Shorter sprigs work best at the front.*

2 *Add the roses and crab-apple stems at random, filling the space between the front and back evenly. Fill any gaps with hawthorn, japonica, elder leaves and buckthorn.*

3 *Finish the display off with a couple of shiny pomegranates to give the arrangement a real harvest feel. These should perch quite happily just behind the rim of the basket. In time they will dry out, but they will still look good.*

85

A mixture of dried materials such as poppy seedheads, arbutus leaves and wheat combine wonderfully with fresh oak leaves in a glorious harvest display.

Harvest Glory

A basket of home-grown apples and pears, together with a tray of eggs, gives a warm harvest air to this informal display on a pine dresser overflowing with jars of dried foods. The lovely curving shapes of fresh oak leaves and arbutus leaves, which have been dried to a leathery brown, set off teasels, dried poppy seedheads and warm red rosehips. A few ears of wheat add texture, echoing the subtle colours of the display in the straw basket.

You will need: Small vase, small high-sided basket, 4-5 stems fresh oak leaves, 3 stems dried arbutus leaves, 3 dried teasels, 4-5 dried poppy seedheads, 3-4 stems fresh dog rose with hips, few sheaves dried wheat.

1 *Place a small vase of water into your basket. Then begin to build the display by adding stems of oak leaves and arbutus leaves. These will give the arrangement form and provide a framework to support the rest of the plant material.*

2 *Once you have established the shape of the display, add a few poppy heads at random. Then place a few teasels at the back. These can be quite prickly, so be careful not to hurt your fingers.*

3 *Add a few more poppy heads and fill any gaps with stems bearing bright red rosehips. Finish off by adding a few sheaves of wheat. Check the display for gaps and fill with more sprigs of foliage if necessary.*

Christmas

Even if you don't generally indulge in flowers for the house, do try to budget for flowers at Christmas. It's the one holiday when most of us spend more time at home, which means we can enjoy them to the full. They also create a welcoming ambience for guests.

Christmas flower decorations can be as ambitious or simple as you wish, and there's a wealth of foliage and florists' hot-house flowers to choose from at this time of year. Adorn your home – both inside and out – with seasonal wreaths made from fresh or dried flowers, hips and berries, and evergreen foliage. If you plan to entertain a lot, a long-lasting floral centrepiece for your dining table is a must. And how about a change from the usual Christmas baubles on your tree? Try decorating it with beautifully tied bunches of dried flowers or even a few fresh flowers.

A mantelpiece is the ideal spot for a floral display – a seasonal pot plant such as a gleaming red poinsettia placed at either end of the ledge and an arrangement of spruce in the middle will ensure a colourful presence for many weeks. You might also like to present your Christmas gifts in an unusual and festive way. A large wicker basket decorated with spruce, ivy and sprigs of brightly berried holly and topped with a generous scarlet bow makes a colourful yuletide statement.

ABOVE Use spruce to decorate a simple wicker basket filled with gifts.

OPPOSITE Fresh foliage and gleaming red apples provide an eye-catching decoration for a front door. For the foliage, choose from laurel, protea, ivy and eucalyptus, and add plenty of sprigs of pine cones.

— *Tree Decorations* —

One of the most traditional festive sights is the Christmas tree gleaming with richly coloured baubles. But why stop there when there's a wide range of plant material – both dried and fresh – just waiting to be transformed into stunning decorations for the tree.

Using dried materials, wire bunches of lavender and bundles of cinnamon sticks onto your tree for a stylish look that will also fill your home with a deliciously spicy scent.

Fresh flowers work well too as tree decorations. Try placing sprigs of fresh gypsophila between the branches. They are just as attractive as they fade and dry. Roses and freesias are stunning on the tree, and last well if you give them a steady supply of moisture. Attach small pieces of florist's wet foam soaked in water onto small clips designed to hold candles, then push the flower stems into the foam. *Never* allow the water anywhere near the tree lights.

OPPOSITE Tie small bunches of lavender and cinnamon sticks with tartan and gold ribbons and wire them onto a box tree.

BELOW Adorn your Christmas tree with a selection fresh flowers by arranging them in blocks of damp florist's foam inserted into clip-on miniature candle holders.

—Yuletide Settings—

An elegant tablecentre always sets the scene at special mealtimes, and Christmas is no exception. Take a distinctive theme such as gardening as your starting point. Fill a trug with foliage, berries and dried roses, then add little terracotta pots to hold individual night lights. Or take a large decorative bowl of water and float on flowers that open up flat, such as gerberas. Anemone heads are another possibility here and they come in heavenly, rich colours. Add floating candles along with the flowers to provide a lovely glow while dining.

An exuberant mixture of fruit teamed with lustrous red roses and plenty of variegated ivy looks thoroughly festive. Go to town with your table by continuing the theme at each place setting. A simple bloom tied with net, a few sprigs of ivy, or a shiny red apple hollowed out to make space for a small night light may be all that it takes.

You can never go wrong with a neat floral display for your centrepiece for the table. A low arrangement of red roses or carnations accompanied by trails of ivy or some other evergreen foliage is both festive in spirit and a traditional display. Or fill a large glass bowl with a mixture of brightly coloured Christmas-tree baubles and stud these with seasonal blooms. To keep them fresh, always give the flowers a good long drink and spray the flower heads with water before arranging them.

If you are feeling really ambitious, try decorating your candle holders with fresh flowers too. Candle cups are ideal for this purpose and are available from florists (see page 101).

One word of warning. Beware of making your table arrangement too tall. If it is higher than eye level when everyone is seated, they will not be able to see anyone on the other side of the table! And if your arrangement takes up too much room, there might not be enough space for the food.

BELOW LEFT Tiny terracotta pots holding night lights, dried red roses and fresh sprigs of holly fill a wooden trug.

BELOW Individual gerbera heads and floating candles drift serenely in a large glass bowl filled with water.

Seasonal Wreaths & Mantles

A fireplace provides an excellent focal point for floral decorations. Adorn your mantelpiece with trails of ivy or bunches of spruce, interspersed with fruit – oranges are seasonal, and small pineapples would look pretty, perhaps tied round with ribbon. Try using potted ivy or pot plants too, such as a couple of rosy poinsettias standing at either end of the ledge. Or make a fresh flower wreath to hang above the fireplace.

If you prefer a more traditional look, reserve your wreath for the front door to make a welcoming entrance. A simple but effective ring can be made from spruce studded with holly and ivy. Add a few pieces of fruit, a large decorative bow and a few pine cones to make it even more special. Use wall planters filled with festive foliage to transform walls too. Simply pile the plant material high, and hey presto!

Opposite Top Fresh flowers, fruit and spruce make a welcoming wreath.

Opposite Bottom Crown either side of your mantlepiece with a poinsettia plant.

Left Kumquats give this front door wreath an extra special touch.

Below Fill a terracotta wall planter to overflowing with ivy, holly, spruce, laurel, cones and colourful silk poinsettias.

Make your home extra festive with a large wreath made of fresh foliage. It will extend a big welcome to both visitors and passers-by. You can use any foliage you like – pick fresh holly and spruce from the garden and mix it with shop-bought hips and twigs. Top with a big scarlet bow for a dazzling effect.

Festive Wreath

The dried orange slices featured in this wreath are easy to make yourself. Slice an orange into several sections and spread out on a baking sheet. Place in the oven at 150°C/300°F/Gas mark 2 for 30 minutes or in a microwave on high for 6 minutes, turning once after 3 minutes. The slices will still be moist, so leave them to dry naturally for about 2 days before using.

You will need: Sphagnum moss; reel wire; 35cm (14in) double wire wreath frame; florist's stub wire; polythene bag or sack; wire clippers; scissors; wire hairpins or grips; selection of evergreen foliage such as variegated holly, spruce, ivies; 12 dried orange slices; selection hips and berries; 10 cones and 8 walnuts sprayed gold, scarlet ribbon, fine twigs.

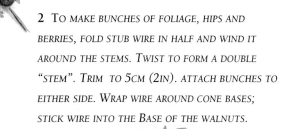

1 *Take a handful of moss and bind it to the frame with reel wire. Build up the moss, tucking each section close to the previous one, until the ring is covered. Make a firm wire loop and attach it securely to the top of the frame. Cut a strip of polythene from your bag to fit the base of the mossed ring and attach to base with hairpins or grips (this will protect the door when hung).*

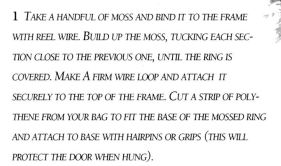

2 *To make bunches of foliage, hips and berries, fold stub wire in half and wind it around the stems. Twist to form a double "stem". Trim to 5cm (2in). attach bunches to either side. Wrap wire around cone bases; stick wire into the base of the walnuts.*

3 *Fill in the middle of the wreath with bunches of holly, ivy and more spruce if necessary, then add clusters of berries, dried orange slices, walnuts and cones at intervals. To finish the wreath, entwine with the fine twigs, and tie on the scarlet ribbon. Spray with water and hang on the door. Regular misting will keep the wreath in tip-top condition.*

A wreath made from dried flowers, foliage and spices makes a sublime Christmas decoration. The strong scents of lavender and the sweet aroma of cinnamon bundles mingle together, making sure that your wreath will smell as good as it looks. If stored carefully, the wreath will last for at least two seasons.

Wreath to Keep

Christmas wouldn't be Christmas without a festive wreath. But if you can't justify buying or making a fresh foliage one, create a decorative ring using dried flowers and foliage. It will last a long time – at least for another season.

You will need: 35cm (14in) double wire frame, sphagnum moss, florist's string, 24 sprigs eucalyptus each about 18cm (7in) long, florist's wire, 30 dried red roses, 24 cinnamon sticks each about 15cm (6in) long, bunch dried lavender cut to 20cm (8 in), 18 pine cones, raffia, tartan ribbon about 4cm (1½in) wide tied into 3 bows, bun moss.

1 *Pad the wire frame with sphagnum moss and secure with florist's string. Or, if you prefer, you can buy a ready-made cane wreath or dried foam ring from florists.*

2 *Wire 8 bunches of 3 eucalyptus sprigs each by twisting florist's wire around the stems. Cut off the rose heads, leaving 5cm (2in) stems, and wire 6 bunches of 5 roses each using florist's wire. Wire 3 bunches of 8 cinnamon sticks together in the same way. Wire 6 generous bunches of lavender. Twist florist's wire around the bottom scales of the cones. Tie raffia around the cinnamon sticks to hide the wire .*

3 *Assemble the wreath by arranging the flowers and foliage at three points on the ring. Start with the eucalyptus foliage and lavender bunches, pointing the stems toward the middle of the ring. Push the wire through the ring and bend the end to secure. Add the roses, cinnamon sticks and cones. Wire the tartan bows and add to each flower clump. Cover the rest of the wreath with bun moss, using a piece of florist's wire bent in half and secured as before. To hang the wreath, wrap strong florist's wire around the top of the wreath and make a hook at the back.*

Materials and Equipment

You don't need much equipment to create even the most stunning of flower displays. But there are a few essentials you will want to keep in your cupboard.

A good sharp knife, secateurs and scissors for cutting and trimming are, of course, important, and sometimes garden canes for supporting larger, architectural type flowers may be necessary. Wires are also often used to ensure that flower heads and foliage stay exactly where they ought to be, while florist's foam and, for heavier flowers, florist's spikes allow you to keep stems upright, or very precisely angled, as if by magic.

For the finishing touches to some types of arrangement, choose from the many different types of ribbons and bows that are available. For a more natural look and its wonderful textural qualities, you should also consider using raffia.

Flower arranging is all about creating a particular mood in a particular setting. To carry this vision through to becoming a reality, the right container is an absolute must. And there are so many to choose from, and in such an extensive range of contemporary or classical styles and materials that you really are spoiled for choice! You can also transform most containers using double-sided sticky tape and a range of dried and fresh plant material. Simply wrap the tape around the container, then stick on leaves, moss and so on. (See also containers on page 14.)

SCISSORS Although some flower arrangers use scissors for cutting and trimming stems, it is probably best to reserve them for removing damaged heads, trimming discoloured foliage and cutting ribbons and raffia for the decorative touches. Choose a well-balanced pair of scissors with an adequately wide grip for the size of your hand, and ones that feature good leverage on the cutting edges in case you need to use them for more heavy-duty tasks.

SECATEURS For cutting through thick, woody stemmed foliage, a pair of sharp secateurs is an essential part of the flower arranger's kit. Make sure you keep both the cutting edge and the flat surface it closes against clean, for ease of use and to avoid leaving a ragged edge.

WIRE CUTTERS If you use reel wire then a lightweight pair of wire cutters will save you time and effort. Heavy-duty scissors can be used for cutting wire but the sharpened edges will soon become pitted and dull.

KNIFE This is by far the most generally useful cutting and cleaning tool in the flower arranger's arsenal. Jack knives fold back into their handle and are probably the safest to use if there are young children about. Some people, however, prefer a fixed-blade knife, but keep it in a sturdy sheath when it is not in use. In most instances, use knives for cutting plant stems in preference to scissors, since a clean slice across the stem is less likely to cause the type of crushing effect that prevents water moving up the stem to the flower head.

FLORIST'S FOAM This is a lightweight synthetic spongy material that can be cut to fit any shape of container. There are two types of florist's foam. Green foam is used for fresh

flower arrangements and must be soaked in water before using. Grey foam is for dried flower displays. Both will support flower stems. They are available from florists in a variety of shapes and sizes – in brick shapes for low arrangements, cylinder shapes for high ones, and cones and spherical shapes for more fancy designs.

MOSS Bun, reindeer, sphagnum, lichen, and many other types of moss can be used as decorative touches and to disguise the constructional aspects of a flower arrangement and wreaths.

WIRE MESH Although fiddly to use, lengths of wire mesh can be easily moulded by hand into any shape and inserted into a container to provide support for flower stems.

FLORIST'S SPIKES (PINHOLDERS) These useful devices sit in the bottom of your container and are available in different sizes and shapes. The most stable types are made of metal and have a series of upward-pointing spikes to pierce the ends of flower stems. Plastic spikes are also available but these don't offer the degree of stability that is often required.

PRONGS You fix these small plastic discs to the bottom of your container with adhesive clay or tape and the upward-pointing spikes help to keep a block of florist's foam firmly in place.

CANDLE CUPS For tall, vertical arrangements unusual containers can be used, such as candlesticks fitted with candle cups. This gives you the option of arranging flowers and foliage in a downward-flowing cascade as well as supporting other stems vertically to give height and movement. Candle cups are shallow, bowl-like containers with a short stem or knob underneath that fits into any narrow-necked base. Wine bottles and narrow-necked vases can also be fitted with candle cups.

BOWLS Bowl-shaped containers of varying size, colour and finish should not be overlooked for many styles of arrangement.

STUB WIRES These sturdy lengths of wire can be easily bent into hairpin shapes, for example, to anchor individual flowers in position, or wrapped around the stems of flowers to tie them into convenient bunches. Cut lengths of stub wires are also often used to fix cones and seed heads in position. They come in a range of gauges and lengths.

REEL WIRE Long lengths of spooled wire that can be cut with wire cutters to any suitable length. The wire is green coloured so does not draw too much attention to itself.

GARDEN CANES These are often used when arranging large-headed specimens that require extra support. Thin canes can also be inserted into hollow-stemmed flowers to keep them rigidly upright.

STRING OR ROPE Use green string or rope to secure decorative features such as driftwood into position. It can also be discreetly placed to act as a fixing point for stub wires. Choose the thickness most suitable for the job you need it to do.

RAFFIA Highly recommended for its decorative and textural qualities. Raffia is made from the dried leaves and stems from certain species of palm trees. It is often tied around an arrangement as a decorative finishing touch and to disguise stub wires and reel wire.

RIBBON Ribbon material in silk, satin, cotton in many solid colours and tartans can be used to encompass a flower arrangement and for tying decorative bows. You could always use a remnant of material you already have at home – perhaps a piece of the same material used for the soft furnishings in the room in which the arrangement will be placed.

WOODEN PICKS As an alternative to wiring cones and seed heads in place, simply spike them with wooden picks and insert them precisely where they are needed in an arrangement.

ADHESIVE PLASTIC TAPE This material has largely replaced the traditional florist's adhesive clay. The plastic tape comes in rolls with its sticky surfaces sandwiched between sheets of wax paper. Cut off as much as you need, remove the wax paper and attach the tape to the bottom of your container. The upper surface of the tape is also sticky and will secure florist's foam or spikes firmly in place. The tape can also be wrapped around the outside of the container. This provides an ideal adhesive surface for sticking on lightweight plant material in a decorative manner.

Care and Conditioning

With the cost of cut flowers today, it is important to make sure that the blooms we buy look fresh and last as long as possible once we get them home. Good florists will do all they can to maximize the life of their flowers by correctly conditioning them before they go on display. By doing this, the shop life of their stock will be considerably extended and so there is less wastage. Just as importantly, satisfied customers will return time and time again.

Of course, you may have your own garden and grow flowers specifically for cutting and arranging indoors. Even so, garden space is probably limited and you won't want to deplete your reserves too rapidly. Following these few simple tips on when to cut flowers and how to condition them before arranging will help to guarantee a regular supply of fresh cut flowers for the home. And even when flowers have gone over and are a little past their best, when the first signs of wilt become apparent, there are still a few tricks you can use to revive them for an extra few days.

GARDEN FLOWERS

In general, the best time of day to cut flowers growing in the garden is early in the morning. At this time the soil and plants may have taken advantage of a good, saturating dew and the plant will not have been subjected to the inevitable stress caused by the hottest part of the day.

It is difficult to give blanket advice on precisely what stage of development flowers ought to be cut, since there are always going to be exceptions. However, as a rule of thumb, cut when just one or two blooms are fully open and the buds are not tight and green but just showing a little colour. Whatever you do, don't leave them out of water for longer than you have to. Have a bucket of water by you to stand them in before arranging. More specific advice on when to cut particular species will be found, where relevant, in the entries in the Flower Guide (see pages 104-9).

CONDITIONING GARDEN AND FLORISTS' FLOWERS

The idea behind conditioning flowers is that you prepare the stems so that the maximum amount of water can travel upward, unhindered, to feed and nourish the heads. Florists' flowers should already have been conditioned, but even so you will need to get them home as soon as possible, since the longer they spend out of water the more quickly they will wilt. So get them home immediately, find a cool spot and stand them in deep water while you decide on how best they should be arranged.

The first stage of conditioning garden flowers, or those bought from a florist that have not been well prepared, is to remove all foliage that will be submerged in water in the final arrangement. It is also a good idea to remove any other foliage that is not essential to your design – leaves compete for water and so deprive the flower heads. They are also likely to decay and pollute the water, reducing the life of the flowers. If you are using a glass vase, they also look unattractive and spoil the look of the display. If your arrangement calls for a lot of foliage, then break off sprigs of leaves and place them separately in the water.

Most species will benefit from having the bottom of their stems cut cleanly with a sharp knife at quite an acute angle. This exposes the maximum possible area of cut stem to water. Never smash stems, as this damages the structure of the stalk, making it more difficult to take up water. It does not help prolong the life of the blooms. For plants with jointed stems, such as carnations, cut just above the joint to prevent air bubbles inhibiting water uptake.

Some cut flowers – daffodils and hyacinths in particular – excrete slime when cut. The slime can be harmful to other flowers. To overcome this, cut the stems of your flowers to the desired length, stand them in a bucket of water overnight, and then incorporate them into your arrangement. Do not re-cut the stems. Alternatively, use flower food that is specially formulated for mixed displays that include daffodils. Poinsettias, poppies and euphorbia, for example, produce a milky white substance, and to stop this flowing you need to hold the bottom of each cut stem briefly in the flame of a candle.

Most hollow-stemmed species tend to wilt quickly once cut, and so the primary conditioning treatment is designed to ensure the flower head receives the maximum amount of water. To achieve this, turn each flower upside down, carefully fill the stem with water and then plug the bottom with a tiny wad of cotton wool.

ENCOURAGING AND REVIVING BLOOMS

To get the most from your blooms, always add flower food to the water. This contains food to feed the flowers and a disinfectant to prevent decay. If you don't use flower food, you will need to change the water in the vase regularly and re-cut the stems. Many florists now include a sachet of flower food with any purchase, and flower food can also be bought separately.

Always use tepid water for your arrangements. It contains the least amount of air – too much air in the water can block the stems and prevent water flow – and will prevent your flowers from receiving a shock to the system.

Flowers such as roses and gladioli may open a little more quickly if you place their stems in warm water. If it seems likely that the flowers have been picked too early and the flower buds are probably too tight to open, pick one or two of the topmost buds and the increased nourishment finding its way to those that remain may encourage them to open. Roses can also be encouraged to open fully somewhat quicker if you blow softly into the opening flower to release the petals gently.

Unfortunately, some cut flowers, especially flowers from the garden, will start to look a little tired after a few days, even if they have been properly conditioned. All is not necessarily lost, however. Wilting soon after cutting or buying flowers is most caused by an air block in the stem, so your initial remedial action is to re-cut the stems under water, removing about 1-2in (2.5-5cm). If soft-petalled flowers are just starting to look a little flaccid, then a quick reviving treatment that sometimes works is to mist the flower head with tepid water.

If foliage and more robust flowers, such as roses, are beginning to wilt, remove the affected stems and float them in a container of water. The more delicate greenhouse-reared roses tend to wilt relatively quickly. Tulips carry on growing after they have been cut. They can grow up to 5cm (2in) and always bend towards the light. I love the look of their long sinewy stems, which gives more character to the display. If you do want to prevent them from turning, wrap the blooms tightly in paper and stand them in a bucket of water overnight. This will make them continue their growth in an upright direction only.

Some blooms are susceptible to ethylene gas, which is emitted by mature fruit and fading blooms. Dianthus, gerberas and irises are particularly sensitive to this, so avoid placing them close to your fruit bowl.

Nearly all cut flowers will last far longer, and require less remedial attention, if you check that the container always has plenty of water. Also, to help extend the life of your arrangement, place it in a cool, draught-free position away from strong, direct sunlight.

Acacia

Mimosa

Attractive, silvery coloured, fern-like foliage and ball-like clusters of tiny, brilliant yellow flowers. The scent of mimosa is much valued by both gardeners and flower arrangers. Requires a draught-free spot indoors away from cold. Cut stems at a diagonal to help water take-up. Cut or buy when the small flowers are just beginning to open and there are no signs of pollen production.

Agapanthus

African lily

Round umbels of dark blue flowers on a tall, foliage-free stem. A valuable plant for flower arrangers because of the strength of its blue colour. Lasts well in water but petals tend to shed.

Alchemilla

Lady's mantle

Small clusters of yellow-green flowers held on graceful, arching stems. The rounded lobe-like leaves are covered in silky hairs and are also used in arrangements.

Allium

Ornamental onion

Rounded heads of tiny star-shaped florets held on long, stately stems. Available in blue, purple, pink and white. They make long-lasting cut flowers, but it is advisable to remove the foliage, which has a distinctive onion smell when bruised. Requires frequent water changes.

Alstroemeria

Alstroemeria, lily of Peru

Very free-flowering, trumpet-shaped blooms borne in rounded heads. A good range of colours available, including orange, yellow and pink. The lance-like leaves are also attractive. Popular with flower arrangers because they last well when cut. Colours tend to fade as the flowers age. Best to buy or cut when one flower is fully open and all buds are showing colour.

Anemone

Anemone

Open, cup-shaped flowers often in strikingly strong colours. They last moderately well as cut flowers if the stems are kept in open water. Do not do well when stems are inserted in florist's foam.

Anethum

Dill

This aromatic herb, well known for its culinary uses, also bears attractive small yellow flowers. Cut or buy when all the flowers are open but do not drop when the plant is gently shaken.

Antirrhinum

Snapdragon

Long-lasting as cut flowers if excess foliage is removed. Good range of colours, including white, crimson, orange, yellow and pink, making them popular with arrangers. Flowers are borne on moderately tall spikes. Buy or cut only when the flowers are completely open.

Aquilegia

Columbine

Available in blue, white, red and yellow, these small, distinctively shaped flowers have a full, bonnet-like front with a spur behind. Not often commercially grown for cut flowers, since they do not last well when transported, but they are long-lasting if cut and used fresh from the garden.

Aster

Michaelmas daisy

These familiar daisy-like flowers are popular with flower arrangers because of their longevity when cut. Available in a wide range of colours, including violet, blue, pink and white. The ends of the stems take water up better if they are cut across diagonally. Cut or buy when most of the flowers are open.

Astilbe

Astilbe, false goat's beard

Best used freshly cut from the garden, where they prefer a moist, water-side position, these attractively feathery plumes last for several days.

Bouvardia

Bouvardia

Small, fragrant, tube-shaped flowers available in white, yellow or red. Best cut or bought when some flowers are fully open and all the buds are showing colour.

Buddleia

Buddleia, butterfly bush

Fragrant flower spikes in white, mauve, purple and red. Long-lasting as cut flowers.

Buxus

Box

Excellent, small-leaved foliage plant giving dense coverage. The fresh, green foliage dulls to more of a yellow colour with age.

Calendula

Pot marigold

Large single or double blooms, in brilliant yellow or orange, which associate well in arrangements with most daisy-like flowers. When buying or cutting, check that the petals at the back of the flower are flat and true-coloured and firm to the touch.

Callistephus chinensis

China Aster

A large range of double round-headed flowers in many colours, including red, rose, lavender, white, pink, blue and purple. Scrape the stems and break their ends, rather than cutting, before arranging.

Camellia

Camellia

Large waxy flowers in white, pink, red, crimson and variegated varieties. Petals are attractively ruffled and single and double forms are available. The glossy dark-green foliage is also valued by flower arrangers. Lasts well as a cut flower, even when left out of water for some time. Check the petals for brown spots before buying or cutting.

Campanula

Bellflower, Canterbury bell

As its common name suggests, this species has bell-shaped flowers carried on tall, branched stems. Some varieties bear their flowers on spikes. Colours include white, blue, lavender and pink.

Carthamus

False saffron, safflower

Orange-coloured flowers with broad, short bracts. Leaves are broadly ovate in shape and minutely toothed. Buy or cut when a few flowers on each stem are partially open and the colour of the remaining buds can be seen.

Centaurea

Cornflower, Bachelor's buttons

Strong-coloured, feathery petalled flowers in a range of colours including blue, white, pink and maroon. Single and double varieties are available. When buying or cutting, flowers should be fully open. Look for strong, rich colours, since the flowers tend to fade with age. Heads may require wiring to keep them upright.

Chrysanthemum

Chrysanthemum

Because of their longevity when cut, these are one of the most popular flowers for arrangements. Both spray and single-flower varieties are available and, apart from blue, virtually every colour can be found. There is also a great diversity of flower shapes, from daisy-like blooms to large spidery and round-headed flowers. Buy or cut spray chrysanthemums when nearly all the flowers are fully open, and check with single-flower types that the flowers are open but the centre of the bloom is still full of unopened petals.

Coreopsis

Tickweed

Broad-petalled, daisy-shaped flowers, usually gold in colour. The stems are spindly but useful for adding height to an arrangement.

Cornus

Dogwood

There are many different species of dogwood, some valuable for their flowers, and others their bracts, foliage or autumn berries. Some species also have wonderfully coloured stems in reds and yellows. Using a sharp knife, make a diagonal cut across the stems to help water take-up.

Cytisus

Broom

Long, narrow green stems bearing small, profuse pea-like flowers. White, cream, yellow, red, lavender and purple colours are available.

Dahlia

Dahlia

With the exception of a good blue, dahlias are available in about every colour. They last moderately well as cut flowers and there are varieties with very large flower heads. There is also a great diversity of flower shapes. Cut or buy when the flowers are open and the petals still firm and crisp in appearance.

Daphne
Daphne
Woody stemmed plant bearing sweetly scented dense clusters of small petalled flowers.

Delphinium
Delphinium
The height of the flower spikes of these flowers lend them to large flower arrangements. The most usual flower colour is blue, of which many shades can be found, but white, pink, purple and mauve are also available. For less-grand arrangements, delphiniums produce secondary flower spikes. Cut or buy when all the flowers are open except for the top-most buds.

Dianthus
Carnation
Available in a wide range of solid and variegated colours, from white, through a range of reds and pinks and into the yellows and oranges. The full-petalled flower heads are attractively ruffled. Before cutting or buying, check to see that the petals feel firm and that there is no indication of darkening on the edges of the petals. Check, too, that the leaves are not discoloured.

Dicentra
Bleeding heart
Sprays of heart-shaped flowers in pink or white on arching stems above finely cut, attractively shaped leaves. Good choice for an airy, delicate arrangement and when extra width is required without adding too much in the way of bulk.

Doronicum
Leopard's bane
Long-lasting when cut, this plant bears long stems of yellow daisy-like flowers.

Eryngium
Sea holly
Different species are useful both for their flowers and foliage in arrangements. Flowers often in rosettes or looser clumps, sometimes on tall, branched stems. Leaves can be rich green and sword shaped as well as deeply toothed. The thistle-like flowers are available in greenish-white, blue and violet. Cut or buy when nearly all the flowers are open.

Eschscholzia californica
California poppy
Cup-shaped flowers in a wide range of colours, including yellow, orange, red and pink. The foliage is also attractive, being blue-green in colour and with a delicate, lacy shape. Best cut or bought when the flowers are still in bud.

Freesia
Freesia
Branched stems of tubular, bell-shaped flowers in gentle shades of yellow, white, gold, pink, lavender and orange. Many are sweetly scented. Long-lasting when cut, buy or cut when the topmost flowers are open and the remainder of the buds are showing colour. Make sure there are no empty nubs at the bottoms of the stems.

Fritillaria
Fritillary
Delicate, nodding flower heads in yellow, brown, green and purple, often with deeper, chequered markings. The impressive F. imperialis has large, bell-shaped flowers in red, orange and yellow borne on tall spikes.

Gerbera
Gerbera
Tall, thick stems bearing a single impressively large, daisy-like flower in shades of red, orange and pale pinky-peach. Excellent as cut flowers. Cut or buy when the flower head is fully open but no signs of pollen production are apparent. Pollen is a sign of an older flower that will not last long.

Gladiolus
Gladiolus
Many hybrids are commonly available in virtually all colours, solid and variegated, except blue. Flowers are borne on thick, tall spikes and should last about two weeks as cut flowers. Remove spent florets as the flower ages.

Flowers open from the bottom of the spike. Cut or buy when the very lowest flowers are fully open, with the next tier showing colour strongly. All other buds on the spike should be tightly closed.

Godetia
Godetia
Heads of small poppy-shaped flowers on top of sturdy stems. Available in some orange shades, pinks, crimson, some with edge variegations. Cut or buy when only a few flowers are open and the other buds are showing colour.

Gypsophila
Baby's breath, gypsophila
Long-lasting tiny white or pink flowers carried on arching, spindly branched stems. Very useful for filling in and softening arrangements. Cut or buy when about half the flowers are fully open and the remainder are still in bud.

Hemerocallis
Day lily
Profuse clusters of large, trumpet-shaped flowers in orange, red, maroon, yellow

and gold. Although each bloom lasts only a single day, if you buy or cut stems with many buds, each spent flower can be removed, leaving the others still to bloom.

Hyacinthus
Hyacinth
Heavy, fleshy spikes of waxy textured, bell-shaped flowers in cream, white, blue, pink and red. Cut or buy when the top of the flower spike is still in bud. Do not stand in deep water, and wipe the sap away from the cut stem ends before arranging them.

Hydrangea
Hydrangea
Tiny white, pink or blue individual flowers tightly clustered into very large heads. Mop head and lace cap varieties available. Hydrangeas can be used as a single-flower arrangement or as part of a grander flower design.

Iris
Iris
Tall, fleshy stems bearing flowers of almost every possible colour. Flowers are

arranged with three upright petals and three hanging ones (standards and falls). Miniature irises are also available for smaller arrangements. Bearded irises are probably the most popular with arrangers and although each bloom is short-lived, multi-stemmed specimens will prolong their presence. Remove spent flowers. Cut or buy when lower flowers are just beginning to open and others on the stem are showing a little colour.

Lathyrus
Sweet pea
Between three and six ruffled blooms on each spindly stem, available in pink, salmon, scarlet, crimson, lavender, mauve, purple and white. They are not long lasting when cut, but they are important for their charming flower shape and scent. Cut or buy when the lowest flower on each stem is just about open.

Liatris
Gay feather
Very long-lasting as cut flowers, these plants bear

round, purple-shaded flowers on narrow spikes. However, unlike most flower spikes, liatris blooms open from the top downward. Cut or buy when the topmost flowers are starting to open and the others lower down are still in bud.

Lilium
Lily
This is an enormous genus of plants with a similar habit consisting of tall, heavily perfumed spikes of trumpet-shaped flowers that are available in virtually all colours, with the exception of a true blue. Some are flecked with other colours. As the flowers open it is advisable to remove the anthers to prevent the pollen falling and staining carpets and soft furnishing. Cut or buy when all the flowers are still in bud but are showing their true colour. Tight buds will probably not open once cut.

Limonium
Statice
Plumes of delicate, paper-like flower heads in lavender, red, pink, white, yellow and

purple. Cut or buy when the tiny individual flowers that make up the heads are just about open.

Molucella

Bells of Ireland

Although the tiny white flowers of this plant are insignificant, it is valued by flower arrangers looking for a mass display of a single species because of its distinctive green, shell-shaped calyces. Long-lasting as a cut flower. Cut or buy when the flowers are open. Remove foliage in order to reveal flower colour.

Monarda

Bee balm, bergamot

This is a delightful, old-fashioned herb, which lasts very well when cut. It has spiky, crown-like flowers in red, pink or lilac and an attractive fragrance.

Muscari

Grape hyacinth

Small bell-shaped flowers in white or bright blue, hanging from short, sturdy stems. Long-lasting when cut.

Narcissus

Daffodil

Best known for their large, golden-yellow trumpet-shaped flowers, daffodils also come in white and pink forms and dual-coloured varieties. Cut or buy when the buds are showing colour. Wipe the sap from the cut ends before placing them in water. Slime emitted from the stems is harmful to other flowers. Either use a special flower food which neutralizes the slime, or cut stems and leave in a vase of water on their own for 24 hours before adding to your display.

Nerine

Guernsey lily, nerine

Moderately long stems of pink trumpet-shaped flowers. Flowers open in sequence to extend their life as cut flowers. Cut or buy when flower buds are just starting to open.

Nicotiana

Flowering tobacco plant

Delicate trumpet-shaped flowers in white, rose, pink, crimson and lime green on moderate to tall stems. The petals are arranged to make a five-pointed star shape.

Paeonia

Peony

Some yellow varieties are available, but they are most often found in shades of pink, rose and red, as well as white. As well as having large, open-petalled flowers, which make them eminently suitable for traditional, oriental-style arrangements, the foliage is also very useful in arrangements. Always remove foliage below the waterline as it will decay quickly. Cut or buy when the buds are fat and are showing their true colour but before any have opened.

Papaver

Poppy

These short-stemmed flowers are available in red, white, pink and salmon with prominent stamens in contrasting yellow. *P. orientalis* has attractive black blotches at the base of its petals and some varieties have black stamens. Although not very long-lasting when cut, their useful life can be prolonged by briefly singeing their cut stem ends in the flame of a candle. Cut or buy when the flower petals are just starting to unfurl.

Rosa

Rose

There are so many different roses it is impossible to do other than briefly mention some of the highlights. As well as the floribunda varieties, there are also the well-known hybrid teas, spray, climbers and old-fashioned varieties. Single, semi-double and double flowers are available, many highly scented, and some with thornless stems. Virtually any colour and shade can be found, as well as variegated forms. The old-fashioned roses are also valued for their lovely autumn hips. Once cut, stand roses overnight in deep water before arranging and remove all leaves and thorns that will be submerged when arranged. Cut or buy roses when buds are showing their true colour. If the necks of the flowers are bent or the buds too tightly closed, the flowers are unlikely to open.

Rudbeckia

Coneflower

These are very popular flowers with arrangers. One of the best-known species is *R. fulgida* (black-eyed Susan), which has yellow, daisy-like flowers with a brilliantly contrasting central cone in black. Cut or buy when one or two flowers are fully open and the others are on the point of opening.

Scabiosa

Scabious

Long-lasting as cut flowers in shades of blue, white, mauve and violet. Cut or buy when the flowers are already open, or are on the point of opening, and the centre of the flowers are full and puffy.

Schizostylis

Kaffir lily

Attractive, long-lasting cup-shaped flowers borne on gladiolus-like stems. These flowers open from the bottom of the spike upward, so cut or buy when one or two lower flowers are open and buds further up the spike are showing their true colour.

Syringa

Lilac

Many shades of flower colour in purple, lavender, lilac and crimson as well as white. Although the individual flowers are small, they are massed into large pyramidal-shaped heads. Cut stems at a diagonal before arranging to encourage water to travel up to the flowers, and remove all lower foliage.

Trachelium

Trachelium

The half-hardy species make long-lasting cut flowers. Useful for small-scale arrangements. Cut or buy when one or two of the individual flowers making up the flower head are open and the other buds are showing colour.

Tulipa

Tulip

Waxy, deep cup-shaped single flowers borne on a single fleshy stem. Many colours are available, either solid or with flecks, stripes, edge variations, veinings and spots. Popular colours include orange, bronze, white, pink, salmon and a purple so deep it appears almost black. Tulips when cut grow toward the light. To keep them upright, wrap them tightly in paper and stand in a bucket of water overnight. Tight buds will not open, so buy or cut when petals are just opening or when buds are showing their true colour strongly.

Zantedeschia

Arum lily, Calla lily

These are bold, dramatic flowers, with a large, white trumpet-shaped flower borne on a glossy green, stout stem. When buying or cutting, check that there is no blackening at the edges or centre of the spathe, which should be firm and smooth.

Index

Acknowledgments

PHOTOGRAPHY CREDITS

a = above, *b* = below,

l = left, *r* = right, *t* = top

p8 Tim Imrie, p9 *l* Di Lewis *b* Lucinda Symons, p10 William Douglas, p11 Theö Bergstrom, pp12-13 Michelle Garrett, pp14-16 Di Lewis, p17 Tim Imrie, p18 Theö Bergstrom, p19 Tim Imrie, pp20-1 Derek St Romaine, pp22-4 Di Lewis, p25 Tim Imrie, p26 Di Lewis, p27 Lizzie Orme, p28 Tim Imrie, p29 *l* Lizzie Orme *b* Derek St Tomaine, pp30-1 Lizzie Orme, p32 Lucinda Symons, p33 Theö Bergstrom, p34 Di Lewis, p36 Andrew Sydenham, p38 Di Lewis, p39 *l* Di Lewis *b* Derek St Romaine, pp40-1 Mary Rose Loyd, p42 Lizzie Orme, p43 *l* Michelle Garrett *b* Di Lewis, p44 Michelle Garrett, p45 Tim Imrie, p46 Theö Bergstrom, p48 Di Lewis, p50 Tim Imrie, p51 *t* Di Lewis *l* Tim Imrie, pp52-3 Tim Imrie, p54 *r* Andrew Sydenham *a* Tim Imrie, p55 Tim Imrie, p56 Michelle Garrett, p57 Di Lewis, p58 Debbie Patterson, p60 Andrew Sydenham, pp62-3 Di Lewis, pp64-5 Theö Bergstrom, p66 Tim Imrie, p67 Mary Rose Loyd, p68 Lizzie Orme, p69 *a* Jerry Tubby *l* Di Lewis, p70 Theö Bergstrom, p72 Andrew Sydenham, p74 *a* Di Lewis *r* Trevor Richards, p75 Lucinda Symonds, pp76-7 Theö Bergstrom, p78 *t* Tim Imrie *b* Lucinda Symons, p79 Jerry Tubby, p80 Di Lewis, p81 Theö Bergstrom, pp82-3 Michelle Garrett, p84 Derek St Romaine, p86 Di Lewis, pp88-9 Di Lewis, p90 Tim Imrie, p91 Trevor Richards, p92 Lizzie Orme, p93 *l* Dominic Blackmore *r* Lizzie Orme, p94 *t* Jerry Tubby *b* Tim Imrie, p95 *t* Trevor Richards *b* Di Lewis, p96 Dennis Stone, p98 Trevor Richards.